Finance Tips & Tricks for Property Developers

AUSTRALIAN EDITION

Contents

1	Lenders	3
2	Structures	10
3	Products	22
4	Packaging a loan proposal	41
5	Raising equity funds	56
7	Equity partners	59
8	Securities	61
9	Glossary of Terms	81

Introduction

Finance is an essential part of any property development project. It can be important for various reasons, but it's necessary for property developers with a higher capital requirement. One explanation for this is the sheer number of expenses for each stage of the project in question, such as capital for council approval, long-term finance to hold and operate the development, and more, as many of these will often need funding. In addition, the existing equity held by developers is usually not significant enough to cover everything from start to finish.

While many moving parts will need consideration, nothing will proceed without proper financing. The type used will need to be compatible with several aspects of the development and have fair and flexible terms and conditions to allow the developer to bring their ambitions for the property to life.

Keeping in mind, it's a wise for developers to get the appropriate finance before committing to a project. A developer will need to understand different levels of finance, each of which is vital to getting funding. We'll discuss each to give you a better idea of what they mean and how they can help you.

From the loans and security to current market trends. While not every developer will access capital (or do so for every project), the good news is that there can often be enough money within the offered interest and terms to make a project work.

The essential aspect of securing finance is understanding the project, its potential, which lender and how to present your plans to maximise your chances of efficient approval. When looking for the correct funding, it's often best to negotiate with multiple lenders; after all, you won't know whether your application is successful until the loan committee has decided, which can take quite time.

1 Lenders

Choosing a lender

In most cases, before talking to a lender. A brilliant piece of advice is to get in touch with the lender or brokerage first to find out about project security before meeting with real estate agents. Confirm:

▸ Type of property you want to build

▸ Location of the development

▸ Potential that a lender can offer with their loans

▸ Lender quoted interest rate, charges and loan term.

If the response is satisfactory on each of the above, here are a few questions to ask yourself:

▸ How much of the total development cost will be covered by financing?

▸ How much equity is needed?

▸ Third, how much will construction and the hiring of professionals cost?

▸ Finally, what are the terms of the loan?

Potential problems with a loan.

The terms may not be entirely suitable for your needs, or added requirements, such as a loan extension. Here are a few examples of why a loan may not be the right fit for your development and general considerations to have in mind:

▸ The payment schedule with interest

▸ Personal liability on the loan

▸ The estimate for settlement costs

▸ Compensation for predevelopment fees

▸ The time to get funding.

▸ The drawdown schedule for the construction

▸ A contractor's letter of credit.

▸ The phases of progress payments

▸ The Surveyors approved by the lender

▸ The costs and terms of potential loan extensions

Commercial Lenders

With property development applications, the leading four banks to consider are Westpac, NAB (National

Australia Bank), ANZ (Australia and New Zealand), and CBA (Commonwealth Bank of Australia). There is many other lending companies for large property development projects. Developers must consider and negotiate the loans available, including the different terms and conditions they are likely to be offered.

Corporate borrowing is the term used for when a financial institution lends to a company, whether for residential or commercial purposes. Before deciding, lenders must confirm that the company in question may borrow (based on its memorandum and articles of association). Typically, these are unregulated mortgages unless a small business takes out the loan and residential property used for security.

The opportunity for commercial loans is broad, featuring options available for different businesses. We can offer funding for various needs, from starting up a company to purchasing a factory.

Interest rates vary depending on the amount you borrow and other factors like the type of loan you are taking out and potential risk factors. But this may not always be ideal for development financing, for short-term interest-only loans, where the interest rate is higher than the usual margin.

The interest rate they charge is determined by the potential risk of financing the development in question. A lender is likely to investigate an individual's business plans, completed projects, and past performance to decide how much risk they are taking by awarding a loan.

Savings banks

Finance from these types of lenders is through depositors and funders not too dissimilar to building societies. But, due to lower rates of total home lending over the years, many building societies have developed into general Banks and offer insurance, advisory services, and more. They are the most flexible lenders, making them excellent for various individuals and projects. They often work with residential property managers and suburban development projects. Most of them stay within their local areas, but common for them to branch out nationally, or even country-wide, for suitable projects.

A few downsides, slower application processes than bigger banks (because of manual underwriting) and higher interest rates. But, even with these negatives in mind, they can still be an intelligent choice for various borrowers, thanks to a more positive approach to lending. Another bonus is using common sense to create solutions and compromises that favour both parties.

6

Investment Banks

The Banking Act controls investment or merchant banks as financial intermediaries, providing underwriting, capital raising, and more. They can grant funding for more in-depth and expensive transactions and act as a financial advisor to clients in various circumstances. In addition, they can offer economic opportunities to retail operations, smaller businesses, and even individual customers. These banks can allow capital financing and bridging (although they focus on larger projects).

Superannuation Funds

Like life insurance companies, these funds need stable cash flow situations. Most of the time, these investments are given to long-term property investment projects that offer endless potential for profit and higher capital growth. It may be worth bearing in mind that the need to follow the trust deed and, so, may have a maximum investment of the fund's value for a project.

Private Banks

You will find several well-known private lenders to choose from that can offer capital for larger development projects. It may be wise to investigate the more obscure choices, too, since these could offer a better deal for your unique circumstances (they may even offer financial arrangements that other, larger companies will not).

These lenders are often much more selective about whom they work with, although if you have a good enough project, you could benefit from their help.

Borrowers will often learn about these institutions by being introduced via trusted sources, such as brokers. This way, the investors can often know more about the developer and their track record. In addition, since they are more exclusive, they have faster turnaround times and other benefits.

Offshore Loans

If you are looking for short-term funding, like development or construction loans, offshore finance may be a viable choice. However, it will not always be the best choice for long-term investments because of the difficulties that currency fluctuations can often cause.

Ideal for overseas investors, most offshore financing options are available for competitive prices and offer enticing sums of money. As a result, many benefits come with these lenders, from their great interest rates to dedicated support.

In addition, as international companies, the applications are from individuals or companies with global properties. They can often work with local customers and many investors, which can benefit those who have income streams from abroad. Overall, individuals or companies who want to invest outside their residence will find offshore loans attractive.

Trust Companies

During the crusades, in the 12th Century, the Law of Trusts was first developed. It came about because the "common law" was indivisible property like Roman law and civil law before it. So, the Lord Chancellor had the power to declare who the actual owner was if it seemed unfair to someone with the legal title to keep it over another person.

With the Crusades, when landowners went to fight, they would give temporary ownership of their property to another person to manage – although when they returned, many of those individuals refused to give the property back. There was nothing that a Crusader in this position could do since common law did not recognise this as a legitimate claim. In the eyes of the law, the property and land belonged to the trustee. Crusaders would petition the king, referring to the Lord Chancellor. He would decide based on his conscience. The concept has not changed throughout the years.

In the modern world, a trustee appoints the trust deed to hold an asset for the beneficiaries, according to whatever terms are in the document. With more complex trust, trustees will often borrow money for a specific purpose, up to set limits. This could, for example, be when a trustee wants to arrange a mortgage and buy a property – but before that, a lender will want to make sure that the trustee has the power to borrow. Not every trusts grant this privilege.

A unit trust is a modern form of pooled investment made under a trust deed. The unit trust is an opportunity to get a greater return than could have been received elsewhere (with the ability to invest a lump sum of cash into the trust and make regular contributions, or both).

Real estate investment trusts offer their benefits since they are a tax-efficient choice for property investment that can allow private investors to work on a project while avoiding the pitfalls of direct property investments. These are not to be confused with mutual fund operators, which are investments that only work with portfolios of shares and cannot be invested into the property industry.

The unit trust companies will only invest in certain shares on the stock exchange and, as a result, differ from most other financial structures since the trustee divides the property into units and allows beneficiaries to subscribe to the teams (like shareholders subscribing to a company's shares). Unit trusts offer security and certainty. Since they offer fixed amounts to beneficiaries based on how much they hold, making them more appropriate than discretionary trusts. There are other benefits to unit trusts, such as discounts on capital gains tax, assets protection, estate, succession planning and more.

Syndicates

These funds allow investors to get involved with exceptional quality properties via a property membership, reducing risks and offering the best features of property ownership.

This form of investment will give the investor ownership over multiple properties. Because of this, syndicates have many unitholders in a private company. They are making it somewhat like a joint venture. You may join a syndicate as a flexible investment option, as unitholders can have over one project and are not required to be there at the end of the development phase.

Another benefit is that they reinvest profits until the syndicate has ended. It can be an intelligent choice when considering the potential for higher returns on collective assets. A unitholder can sell their shares to other members (or new members) if they wish.

In the right situations, a syndicate can give an investor

the chance to put their money into a fantastic property without the hassle of full ownership or to invest in a large-scale commercial project that may not have been possible under other circumstances. Here are the more attractive features:

- ▸ Investors can buy higher value properties with reduced capital

- ▸ Being part of a syndicate gives investors the ability to spread the risk over multiple properties

- ▸ By diversifying your assets, you can have more stable returns and reduce volatility

- ▸ The suitable investment could allow you to get more out of it for less effort, as well as safe time in other ways, too

- ▸ While there are several advantages, there are downsides that you should know about, such as

- ▸ Because there are multiple investors, you will not have complete control when deciding about the development.

- ▸ There are several considerations for the other investors, from their monetary interests to their goals with the project. As a result, this may hide their intentions or change them later than their objectives and financial situations vary.

▸ Like with real estate and other forms of investment, there are still a few economic situations that can pose a risk to your project, like fluctuations in the property market.

Joint Venture Agreements

One of the many available methods of getting funding for development is joint ventures. The way joint ventures work is where an investor or lender enters a partnership with a developer and funds the project (from purchasing the land to other requirements) for a share of the profits down the line. Alternatively, the lenders take a fewer hands-on approach and might sign a contract with the developer, buy the land, and earn a percentage of the profits. The prospect of entering a joint venture alongside a developer is appealing. This funding takes many forms but depends on the project at hand.

In either scenario, the basic premise remains; a developer and a lender come together, one offering an idea and the skill to execute it and the other with the cash to fund said idea. Two people come together, each with something different to offer, to run a single project and contribute in their way (whether through the development work itself or via funds).

In these types of loans, an investor will first assess the potential risks and liabilities of any parties involved. It is always important to consider whom you are going into a joint venture with, as their liabilities could reduce your chances of getting a loan (or harm your borrowing capacities or interest). On the other side, if they have a better financial history than you, there's a chance that they could help to improve your borrowing capacity, which could be worth keeping in mind when you are choosing whom to work on your joint ventures.

These forms of funding can involve two or more people buying a property. They could be business partners or even just friends and family, entering a long-term arrangement with other individuals — which must be made clear to the borrowers at the beginning. Because of this, it can be vital for the terms of the agreement to be examined and agreed to in writing to prevent any legal complications from occurring later. It is often wise to have an exit strategy if things don't go as planned. After all, a person's situation, finances, and personal circumstances can vary over time or even throughout something short, like a year.

It could be worthwhile to set up a separate loan for each buyer if you are able. Here, if one borrower defaults on a loan and cannot make their repayments, it will not influence your credit history or borrowing capacity. Plus, even if the loan runs, separating them can be beneficial in other ways, like counting against loan services where the lender collects unpaid interest, principal, etc. Without separate loans, the entire debt would matter even though there's somebody else paying a part of it. You may choose to invest with a group of people. If so, everybody must agree on how the project will be treated and a workable exit strategy before.

It's essential that all individuals have the same goals in mind, a few of which can include:

▸ Whether you want to hold or sell the development.

▸ Try to keep a modest LVR (Loan to Value Ratio) to boost cash flow.

▸ Consider if you're going to refinance or continue to pay off the current loan.

▸ Does everyone involved want to earn a higher short-term cash flow or add capital value?

Company

If you dig through history, you find that the first company formation dates to the Dutch expeditions to East India and that their methods have been similar since the early 1600s. In that year, they undertook a certificate of incorporation for record-keeping. Finally, they went public, which allowed them to raise a high number of guilders (around 6.5 million) to help divide the risks of their expeditions and allow local investors to earn a profit.

In mortgage applications, they assess public company directors as employees. Directors of smaller firms are sometimes given ownership of a set percentage of the shares and considered as self-employed individuals in most cases. Since shareholders own the company, they can control the distribution of profits. They will still receive the same pay and documentation as any other employees would.

As a result, common for directors to arrange their income to receive smaller salaries. Although it can be less stable than a regular employee, it can be more challenging for many company directors to get and sustain a mortgage. Not only that, but when company accounts are constructed to minimise tax (which can be done by showing the least amount of money available for taxation), it does not accurately reflect the company's financial position, which can cause complications.

Many investors choose to utilise a Special Purpose Vehicle (SPV), a business entity with a particular limited purpose, and leave the company's directors under an obligation to guarantee the loan. The property's legal owner is the registered company, and the directors will make sure that they met all the responsibilities of a limited company. Those who would otherwise have taken ownership of the property instead become the company's shareholders, meaning that they own the company and not the property. The restrictions and limits imposed on special purpose vehicles will often depend on the situation and whether the individual can commit the company to borrow.

A financial institution will only lend to a small company if the directors and shareholders agree to settle the debt should the company not meet the predetermined requirements for repayment. but a few advantages can come with buying under a company structure, from planning tax on dividends to higher asset protection outside of the company.

It's important to consider that lenders will often pay close attention to the security on offer, the directors, and that those entering the contract may do so. Because of this, anyone hoping to get financing for their company should first find out if and what they'll be allowed to borrow (as well as other factors that could affect a lender's decision, like a poor credit score).

It's wise to consider that the setup costs can be high with most company structures. Many businesses are not eligible for a discount on capital gains (often only available to trusts or individuals), costing them even more cash. Sometimes, companies cannot distribute their losses, making this structure unsuitable. Alongside this, even if a company director is not considered liable for the business's debts, they will still be held accountable for other responsibilities, like ensuring solvent trading.

Many companies get referred by their tax advisors to source debt and equity, and with our extensive network, we could offer terms that the borrowers (and their tax advisors) are pleased with.

Partnerships

In simple terms, a partnership is an agreement where two or more individuals operate a business together. Unlike a company, they do not consider a partnership as a separate legal entity and so, the partners own the assets and handle any liabilities. It is always best for a partnership to have their agreement in writing, which should detail all the critical aspects of the relationship, from the proportions of profits they share, to how will the company be managed should one partner leave. Those with a significant deal in mind may want to find partners for several reasons, including diversification and reduced risks. Alongside this, more investors can offer more financial resources – and that would be beneficial.

Having a partner might be one of the best decisions for your business. Or it could be one of the worst – although the boosted pool of cash can be handy for those starting in real estate. If you find a partner that complements your skills, you could make the most of the agreement.

It would help if you got an excellent lawyer to create a contract that specifies what will happen should one partner leave the arrangement. A buy/sell agreement is the best choice, since it outlines all the terms and conditions for redistributing assets and allows one member to leave.

There are so many factors that can change a person's life, from moving home to getting divorced, that could cause strain on the partnership. Arguments can ensue when one party leaves, so having an agreement already in place can be vital to protect everybody's interests.

It could be worth remembering that partnership disputes will only line the pockets of lawyers and accountants. The business or owners will not benefit, so there's no way of avoiding a legal agreement.

Many people consider family members to be an excellent choice for a partnership — and although it sounds good in principle, sometimes disputes can occur, especially when a partner involves family members with different goals and plans for the project. To make sure clarity, get the arrangement you are making in writing the same way you would with anyone else.

3   Products

Seed Capital

In certain financial situations, seed capital might be necessary for the concept stages of the development. While this type of finance can be small, they need it to cover the various costs involved in the earlier stages of projects, from paying consultants to submissions for approval. We can consider seed capital a high-risk loan by lenders and, so, is often only obtainable by offering a stake in the project. It comes from personal assets, friends and family, or a private investor interested in high returns on capital.

Land Acquisition loan

As the name implies, this type of financing assists the buy of the land (or a potential development site). A developer's track record and ability to secure debt with assets rely on whether an investor provides a land acquisition loan. It's essential, as most lenders are not keen to fund land-only if the developer has not yet got approval for their desired project. Borrowers should secure the land without debt, since the approval process can often take time. So, it might be costly and further reduce profits because of the interest charged during this time.

Construction Funding

Before submitting a proposal, essential to know the loan providers and their criteria. Since this can be a significant step in securing financing, these things you should keep in mind:

▸ Type of real estate development (which can include the number of lots, style, size, etc.)

▸ Location (both suburb and postcode are vital factors to consider)

▸ Your profile (to show your experience and history as a developer)

▸ The purpose for developing (whether it's intended for trading or holding, for example)

▸ If you want to sell, presales to act as evidence. This might be a policy need or just an obligation from the lender.

Construction loans are interest only, allowing developers to finance the land as necessary. In most cases, we can capitalise the interest during the building period. The rest of the loan (including interest) is often paid off should the borrower sell or refinance.

Lenders advance funds against the loan limit when

advancing construction loans. Although the developer or owner handles the payment, the lender makes the payment as part of the loan agreement to protect their security. It is essential for the lender to report the work completed by its independent Quantity Surveyor.

Most borrowers will need a permanent source of finance secured or at least an exit strategy (via sale to a third party) for a lender to agree to offer funding. But this is not always the case, as lenders may not force developers to rely on their financial strength alone and have other options or requirements.

Bridging Financing

These loans are taken out to close on a property (and sometimes, certain other situations too) and repaid when sold or refinanced. A developer will often take out a bridging loan to carry a project until development approval. Like many others mentioned, the risk factor involved can increase the interest rate and may not be available from most standard lenders. Once the authorisation for construction finance is approved, it will complete the bridging loan and fund the project as planned. It is worth keeping in mind that many bridging lenders out their offer funding outside standard mortgages. They are only available through specialised brokers.

These loans help borrowers buy a property before selling one they already own or pay a tax bill until they receive payment from the property they sell. There are benefits for investors looking to secure finance fast, which can be tough to find in a vast marketplace, especially if you have a more complicated situation on your hands than a standard mortgage.

Case Study

Bridging loan in Sydney central business district

Property details

Within Sydney's central business district and nearby the cobbled streets of the rocks, the real estate was on a historic road, with proximity to major infrastructure and entertainment venues.

What the client wanted

They refused the applicant's finance just days before the settlement date. He was heading towards legal and financial trouble.

Difficulties along the way

After applying, the lodgement of a hefty court judgement alerted the lender on the borrower's credit file.

Key points

Several specialists bridging lenders are out there, many of which can offer funding outside the traditional mortgage, only available through specialised brokers.

What we did

We introduced a specialist lender who prides itself on being efficient at quick settlements.

The results

We settled the transaction one day after the scheduled date. Because we facilitated bridging finance, they incurred increased costs. But the clients understood, and we refinanced them into standard mortgage terms after the court judgment was resolved.

Mezzanine Loan

Private investors or venture capital companies often fund these loans. Developers use this form of funding to secure more financing for their developments if the senior lender requires more equity. The money lent is treated as equity.

Mezzanine loans can often be more expensive for developers. This is because they debts with a higher capital cost. In addition, if the borrower defaults, they repay once they repaid the priority mortgages. If the borrower cannot repay, the lender may convert to ownership or equity interest in the company's project. Mezzanine debt lenders will often want a higher return.

Commercial Bills

Developers can often raise funding through drawing and discounting from negotiable bank bills through this facility. Often, borrowers will have the chance to choose from several facilities, most of which will use the current market techniques to suit a developer's specific needs. In addition, they will have drawdown rates (from to those tailored to their requirements).

There are other factors to consider, like the floating bill rate, which can decide the drawdown rate and duration of the bill. The term of the bill is essential to how the interest rate is determined. Lenders will accept and discount the bills on the required dates, and they will set the drawdown rate for the facility's term. Drawdowns will be fixed, and they will discount the bill before the first drawdown date.

Risk participation financing

Sometimes, a large amount of cash will be needed, or development and a lender might want to reduce their risks (or cannot fund a loan of that size fully). They may assemble a syndicate of other investors to finance the project when this happens. Commonly, the lead lender will take a larger share of upfront fees and coordinate the monthly service fees–and they may even fund the project costs. In most instances, two-thirds of the loan is notional debt, while the rest notional.

Builder's design, construct and finance loan.

A builder may offer a design, construction details, and finance for approved developments if they have a healthy balance sheet. Other factors are often involved, too, like if the builder has extensive work and their level of interest in the finished product. A builder will need an unconditional bank guarantee that all associated costs will be repaid in full on time. This poses several benefits to developers, like not paying for the entire equity from a commercial bank. In these situations, a developer will only need to fund the land and development approval costs (as well as overheads). This form of financing is not perfect, though, as builders will add their margin over their bank's interest rates to cover their risks. You might even find that this will be higher than the average rates you would expect. Before entering this type of loan, best to have an independent quantity surveyor to make sure that all the builder's costs align with the project's needs.

Lenders Assessment

For most lenders, sourcing new business is the responsibility of business development managers. Credit assessors review applications and analysts underwrite to decide whether the transactions are likely approved. On larger transactions, most lenders usually operate a credit committee, which votes on whether an application should be approved or disapproved. A credit assessor does not vote in most cases but only recommends a transaction. Often, they recommend the transaction with certain conditions. They could ask for added security, the amount lowered, the interest rate raised, the term shortened, or the amount guaranteed by the borrower increases. Sometimes loan committees include assessors in regions other than where the property is located. Throughout this book, I have emphasised that not all lenders are the same. As a result, you must consider all the items and decide which are most important to the lenders. In summary, lenders will often focus on three factors: person, purpose, and property – known as the three Ps. In any situation, there are usually several things that a lender will need to address when assessing potential borrowers

▶ Individuals can and cannot borrow financially and in terms of legal barriers.

▶ If and how funds should be allocated to separate entities.

▶ How much should be lent to each applicant?

Any good lending policy will need to consider these factors. Here are a few examples of matters that need to be assessed with individual or company applicants:

▶ The lender's usual strategy, as well as market positioning and business levels, that might have an impact

▶ The profit margins that they would like from providing a loan

▶ The potential risks that come with lending to the applicant

▶ Arrears, recovery statistics and any other relevant circumstances.

For property developers, essential to keep a clean credit report. When reviewing your loan, banks and lenders will contemplate your credit history – and anyone who has applied for finance will have a credit file that will play a huge role in their chances of approval. Debt is a genuine risk that can be hard to overcome, especially for new developers. Even outside of this, one of the most significant roadblocks for beginners is that there can often be little room for negotiation, so how do you choose the ideal one? A good finance broker can often help with all of this, guiding you through the many lenders, loan options and updates on product changes that could be positive/negative for an investment.

When you take out a development or construction loan, a developer should consider the varying bank conditions and how your reputation and track record influence the project. The lender must meet specific requirements before the first advance. A lender's indicative terms are usually described in an offer letter or on an indicative term sheet, and the full terms and conditions are in the facility agreement. Lender conditions and precedents will include, but are not limited to:

▸ Building Contract: An independent quantity surveyor or engineer will need to review the costs and sign a building contract with a reputable builder.

▸ Valuation: This report deals with both the current "as is" value and the gross realisation value of the completed project.

▸ Survey Report: The surveyor's report confirms the dimensions of the land are the same as the title searches and that no encroachment or other boundary problems exist.

▸ Geotechnical/Site History: Besides not being listed on the EPA register, the geotechnical report should confirm that contamination or sub-surface conditions on the property will not affect the project physically or financially.

▸ Searches: Typically, the lenders' solicitors conduct all necessary property searches on the security properties, which they then certify are acceptable.

▸ Residential build projects may need a specific number of conforming presales that equate to a percentage of the total debt. But this can differ depending on the lender and other risks.

Before lenders can decide the associated costs of a loan, they must contemplate a borrower's creditworthiness and receive information on the project itself. The amount a lender will offer will often depend on factors like current economic conditions and any obvious risks from funding the development, which will be determined by: Typically, a lender will consider various terms and conditions to mitigate their losses.

▸ The type of development

▸ Projected sales (at least when applicable)

▸ The form of tenancy (Commercial or residential)

▸ Income streams to service the loan

▸ The financial history of the borrower

▸ Developer's record of accomplishments.

Interest Rate

Borrowing money comes at a cost, and lenders will consider their profit margin before offering any funding. The lender's costs of funds influence the profit margin, how long the funds will be outstanding, and the risk the lender will take. Lenders often reduce their profit margin if a developer has a large balance sheet and reliable customer. Most times, borrowing can either boost gains or cause losses and make the opportunity for returns less worthwhile. For example, the instability caused by interest rate fluctuations on construction loans, interest is charged as interest-only (IO) and capitalised on larger projects, known as prepaid interest or interest in advance, deducted from the loan proceeds at settlement.

Market

Larger markets have better pricing for prime real estate projects. Because of higher rental rates in comprehensive markets, tenants may replace those who vacate the property at the end of their lease term. A significant employer's loss will not affect an entire region's financial standing, so their economies are more stable.

Property type

In the commercial real estate market, retail, office, industrial and apartments have the most readily available financing because of their consistent cash flow, barriers to entry for new competitors and consistently high occupancy rates.

Property quality

A new property that will appeal to tenants and customers soon is more attractive to lenders for many reasons. When leases expire, or tenants move out, easier to re-tenant them. Further, there should be fewer capital expenditures throughout the loan term, so the borrower has more cash flow to take care of debt service and use for other business purposes. Green buildings, which are more energy-efficient and less harmful to the environment, are becoming popular, and they may help lenders decide to price.

Credit quality

For office properties, industrial properties and retail projects, the quality of tenants will affect the lender's pricing. The better the tenant, the less likely they will vacate the space before lease termination and the less likely they will fail. In addition, the tenant's income pays the monthly debt service interest to the lender.

Borrower strength and experience

An experienced borrower and asset position are usually helpful in getting a better price. A large borrower helps the lender make pricing and credit decisions even though the lender is looking at the property to repay the loan first. In addition. Even with a non-recourse loan in which the borrower can walk away from the property. Because when the property needs capital improvements or has a rough patch, the borrower can continue to feed the property with much-needed collateral.

Case Study

Purchase of land for civil construction
Property details

A significant residential development zone Northwest of the central business district in Victoria. The site came with plans and permits for shovel-ready civil construction for approx. One hundred fifty-seven blocks were available, resulting in countless house and land packages and a parcel of established homes.

Key points

Where the LTV exceeds a certain level, the lender may increase charges.

What the client wanted

The clients were Melbourne based and were comparing offers from other lenders. They contacted us seeking reduced upfront costs by our lender being able to offer a higher LTV (Loan to Value Ratio)

Difficulties along the way

A few lenders had scepticism about the near potential future of the site. In addition, the added risk real estate that's non-income producing,

What did we do?

We arranged a meeting with one of our most reliable lenders for land subdivisions.

The results

After credit assessment, we offered reasonable terms with higher Loan to Value subject to presale condition being met. Twelve months on, civil construction begun.

▶ LVR: 65%

▶ Rate: 5% variable rate (interest only)

▶ Term: 2 years

Loan to value

The greater the loan request percentage, the greater the risk to the lender and thus, they may charge a higher interest rate to compensate for the increased risk. The standard practice among lenders is to lend 75 per cent of the property's value. Their constitutions often impose this limit.

Most times, borrowing can either boost gains or cause losses and potentially make the opportunity for returns less worthwhile. For example, the instability caused by interest rate fluctuations on construction loans, interest is charged as interest-only (IO) and capitalised on larger projects, known as prepaid interest or interest in advance, deducted from the loan proceeds at settlement.

Loan to Value Ratio

Abbreviated to LTV or LVR, the Loan to Valuation Ratio as a guide. For both short-term development construction and long-term investment loans. but, this can vary from one lender to another, especially with security and where it is located as rural securities are not as liquid, which results in lower LTVs (Loan to Valuation).

An excellent way to reduce this risk is to minimise your leverage and try to maintain 70 per cent of the overall development costs and 65 per cent of the final asset value. Other issues that might arise:

Presales

One of the biggest hurdles for most developers trying to get funding can be presales, especially for more significant residential developments. A lender will want a certain number of presales to reduce their risks. While the percentage of pre-sold units is not set, funding can vary slightly from one lender to another.

You can often overcome the presales condition, such

as securing standby presales, which can prompt the construction loan to begin at once rather than waiting for all the requirements to be met. If you need help, we could help you find lenders that will offer a loan without presales, although this can depend on the scale of the development and come at a higher cost because of the risks posed.

Case Study

Construction finance in Hawthorn Melbourne

Property details

Two fully detached dwellings side by side were under contract. After demolition, the site was ideal for building multiple townhouses.

What the client wanted

Twelve months from, they did not meet the presale conditions of the settlement, the development approval was given, and the clients were seeking presales to meet their financial conditions. The unforeseen Victorian lockdown prevented mobility, and, as a result, the client could not meet the presale obligations.

Difficulties along the way

Because they did not meet the presale conditions, we resorted to our network of lenders and sourced a suitable financier that accepted the current number of presales.

The results

We worked with the lender and got the project off the ground. The loan attracted a higher interest rate and associated costs because of the lack of presales. but the client was pleased with our success.

4 Packaging a loan proposal

Recently, over the last few years, the packaging of development projects has increased the need for finance. Today, a submission with several types of documentation in a binder just does not get the response you want from lenders. We must lay everything out, from a logical order of documentation, to the overall presentation of the project. All of this takes time and effort.

You must have all your documentation in place for the submission, resulting in a faster loan processing time and boost your chances of getting your loan approved. Preparing the submission can often take weeks between the developer and financiers. Still, the end goal is to create a professional and laid out proposal to maximise your chances of getting approval.

But, many factors will still decide the process outside of this. The guidelines can vary from one lender to another (or for the type of development). Conditions like a borrower's track record and credibility are essential aspects.

If you do not have a track record of experience, hiring an expert who has the ability you need for the project could be beneficial. A skilled project manager could be one of the most critical team members you can have. It might even be worth partnering up with a developer who has an excellent track record to increase the chances of funding.

We aim to assist clients in preparing the best possible loan submission (as well as connect them to the most suitable lenders)

Other charges

In most cases, there are other fees outside of the interest rate, which can simply be another opportunity for lenders to increase their profit margins and reduce risks without having unbearable interest. These can vary between 1-4% (although it can vary depending on the overall potential of the loan).

Construction loan period

The loan period will often be determined by how much time they need to plan construction. Fortunately for developers, most lenders will increase the time frame to allow the borrower to get presales, offering a faster settlement. need

Terms and conditions of the loan agreement

Lenders can ask for other terms and conditions to be met to support the loan (for example, they could require other collateral to secure the development). The requirements that they have can often vary from one to another. So, always best for borrowers to negotiate to achieve a middle ground that everyone can agree on.

Joint and Severally

If multiple borrowers are applying for finance on a project, lenders will often require all the borrowers to sign personal and joint guarantees. In addition, applicants involved must understand that if funding defaults, and the loan is called in, all borrowers will be responsible for their share of the loan and the claims of the other borrowers if they cannot uphold their end of the deal.

Non-recourse debt

This form of loan is a debt by using a pledge of security (specifically, real estate, in most cases). It does not leave the borrower liable if they default – all that occurs is that the lender will seize the property limited to that security.

Since the lender cannot seek any other compensation, even if the property does not cover the value of the defaulted amount, the LTV (Loan to Valuation) ratios are often in the 50-60% range even if the borrower does not have to worry about personal liability.

Recourse or non-Recourse

Lenders want a personal guarantee to secure a loan. They may require partial or complete guarantees. It is in a borrower's best interests to reduce these guarantees as much as possible. Unfortunately, the developers have lost their chance to earn a reasonable profit purely because their guarantees have failed. Here are a couple of things that can reduce the risks.

If other guarantors are required, they share the risk among all parties. The downside is that the developer may have to share equity of the project to be backed by them accept a higher interest rate from the lender to minimise or negate a personal guarantee. but, if the development seems profitable enough, this could be worth considering.

Non-recourse debt is a pledge of security (specifically, real estate, in most cases). It does not leave the borrower personally liable if they default – all that occurs is that the lender will seize the property limited to that security. Since the lender cannot seek any other compensation, even if the property does not cover the value of the defaulted amount, the LTV (Loan to Valuation) ratios are often in the 50-60% range even if the borrower does not have to worry about personal liability. There may be instances where it might be time to consider other financing options (as your debt grows). This could mean putting other properties at risk, such as your home. If this is looking likely for you, you will need to consider both recourse and non-recourse loans from this point forward.

We will use other assets as security against these types of loans and determine the funding for the loan. Besides the borrower's assets, they may pledge other assets as collateral. The bank may feel more comfortable with the debt and lower the interest rate. With private property loans, full-recourse loans are the most popular.

If the bank cannot use the borrower's other assets to cover the shortfall, the bank may offer non-recourse financing if the borrower cannot repay the loan. To protect the risk taken on by the bank by making these loans, they have higher hurdles, not least of which is a higher interest rate. It may be worth noting that this type's property loans are rare in Australia.

Additional collateral

Most lenders would want more than just a personal guarantee, often requiring added security as property or other assets if you default on your loan. It can often be a good idea to keep assets under a separate ownership vehicle and as a separate entity (instead of part of the joint loan's collateral).

When taking guarantors, a lender must exercise great caution. In one sense, it wants to be sure that it takes all legal measures to make sure the guarantor pays. In another, it does not want to take any risks. They must prevent the guarantor from absolving themselves of responsibility,

You will want to guard against the guarantor appealing the guarantee's validity, claiming that they did not explain the terms, or that they were under undue pressure to sign. Therefore, an independent legal opinion is required by every prospective guarantor before committing.

It is common for lenders to ask for additional security on loans should the borrower default on their payments. A guarantee can often take various forms, depending on the situation or just the lender's preferences.

Negotiating on the details of the loan documents

Once you have approached various lenders, it's essential to review and contemplate the terms and conditions of each lender and what the loan offer contains. Most lenders will structure the document to their benefit. It's worth keeping in mind that clauses could be reworded or taken out, whilst others are non-negotiable. Remember that negotiating on the clauses is far more common in development loans than residential mortgages, so don't be afraid to speak up.

Be aware when a lender offers finance because of the project or the developer's experience. It is always essential to have a good relationship with a lender since you're likely to be working with them for quite a long time. In addition, a lender must have complete confidence in the developer's ability to repay the loan.

Prepayment charges

After completing their development project, developers taking out a long-term investment loan should consider what happens once they discharge their loan. For example, will they pay in full before maturity, as most long-term fixed-rate loans will have a prepayment fee if paid off early? This charge will reduce over the loan term. We recommend negotiating for a prepayment fee, not to apply if the lender is notified that they will settle the loan in full.

Fees from banks

Bank fees can contribute to their revenue for many lenders, especially from local and regional branches. Therefore, it's always important to consider the costs involved, and banks will often charge for several items, such as drawdowns on your loan, capital raising fees and more. Therefore, borrowers should always analyse the expenses when they get an offer and see if they can negotiate.

Product fees

▸ It can come at a flat rate or percentage of the overall loan and is sometimes refundable when the loan does not go through.

▸ Establishment fees can be added to the loan if necessary.

▸ Ongoing management fees.

▸ Line Fees.

Application and processing fees

▸ They can often charge commitment fees on mortgages to cover the costs of processing and assessing applications. The fees can vary from one lender to another.

▸ Solicitor Fees.

▸ Valuation

▸ Quantity Surveyor

Higher leverage charges

▸ When the loan to value ratio exceeds the defined threshold,

Advisor fees

▸ Sometimes charged by the intermediatory for mortgage arrangement. This should always be clear in the initial disclosure information.

▸ Comes as a fixed fee, although some may prefer to charge a small percentage of the mortgage advance instead (with non-standard mortgages)

Experienced brokers can use their expertise to waive the initial loan-application fee, form a more suitable loan offer, structure business terms, and offer general professional help. If you choose to work with a broker, always best to find a specialised professional to assist you.

Since there is no set standard for how much finance brokers could charge, always best to ask about their fees upfront and negotiate better costs. Most brokers will have several small expenses, like a success commission based on a set percentage of the loan proceeds (somewhere between 0.05% and 2% depending on the loan size).

Many options allow you to be more creative when structuring your loan, since you can adjust the terms and conditions to suit your requirements. Developers will often have quite a few unique needs based on their project, so a specialised broker and accountant can be excellent at helping reach their expectations. With a broad range of lenders out there looking for a promising project to finance, there is no harm in shopping around until you find the ideal one for you.

It is not always easy to find the perfect development finance solution, as most borrowers don't have enough time, energy, or resources available to them. In these cases, finding the services of a specialised finance broker or other similar professional could be ideal. The best financial brokers offer:

- Extensive knowledge on how to find the best lenders for a client's unique needs

- Information on all the best interest rates and charges on the market

- Expertise on how to present a project and negotiate with lenders

- Time and resources to offer the best solutions to clients

- Experience and relationships with lenders

We are available to discuss your unique requirement for your next project,

support@sherwoodfinance.com.au or 1800 743 796

Potential development project issues

Long lead times

The many factors involved with investments and developments, from buying to selling to investors, could take years. but, the changes to the property cycle could put you in an unexpected position during this time.

You can't subdivide or rezone the land.

If you buy land believing that you could divide it, but the laws and policies on the matter have changed, leaving you with an incomplete project and vacant land.

Angering the locals

When you are going about your development project and planning stages, dealing with citizens who believe that what you are doing is wrong or that it just does not suit the location (they may even find other reasons to complain).

Objections from the council

There are local planning laws and policies to consider. For example, local councils may side with residents on social and economic issues if they are against the project.

Roadblocks that delay your schedule

Even for the most organised developers, projects go along with their planned schedule.

Interest rates and the economy

Developments can often be projects that take a few years

at least, and, in this time, interest rates and the economy can drastically change and cause difficulties for you.

It's not always easy to sell

Regardless of your project, finding out that the market has changed over time could make it difficult for you to on-sell for your expected price. Of course, there is the option to rent instead, and while this can be an excellent real estate vehicle, not the most liquid of investments.

Construction costs

It can be easy for developers to exceed their planned budget, affecting projected profits.

Your builders could go broke.

It's not too uncommon for builders to go broke. Something might not cut the best builders just out for the business side of things, and the industry itself can be tough to manage.

Case Study

Incomplete construction mortgage in Brisbane.

Property details

They neglected a prominent freehold incomplete construction site at a central intersection north of Brisbane because of a shortage of funding from the builder.

Key details

Many lenders will not consider applications for incomplete construction sites because of additional risks.

What the client wanted

A group of experienced investors saw the opportunity to take over and complete the construction work, but they needed access to an appropriate lender.

Difficulty along the way

The vendors' insolvency meant working under strict time constraints to complete the transaction.

What we did

We arranged for a colleague to inspect and forward a detailed report before submitting a formal loan application.

The results

We achieved an ideal result within an unusual lending scenario.

5 Raising equity funds

Equity is a term used for cash at risk, either from the developer or investor, that covers the gap between the loan and the developer's total cost. They consider the value that remains in a property. In these cases, a property owner's equity will be the monetary interest that the owner has that exceeds the remaining mortgage debt. Properties with long-term mortgages will often have less equity because of the amount of interest paid with the monthly repayments.

Many developers in the initial stages of their project will often find that one of the hardest things to do is to find a suitable investor. So here is a little more information on how to prospect for equity funding.

Most of those involved in significant developments where the funding requires extensive financing (with high equity contributions reaching millions) will find that they do not have the resources they need to get the project up and running. A developer in this position should consider their options, like finding a partner and sharing an equity position – and seek referrals from your accountant and solicitors and see if there are any opportunities for partnerships.

If your plans seem promising enough, a solicitor may form financing comparably to a mortgage or equity loan. With equity loans, the investor will become a shareholder. If you choose to do this, always best to have a flexible approach and consider your investment opportunities.

Developers looking to get finance from an investor may only raise part of the total funding. The lender will want cash equity to close the deal, with the developer having to buy the land and deposit a cash equivalent using another property as equity. If the borrower has an excellent financial position, they might even offer equity themselves or get other investors to contribute to close the deal.

Most developers invest their cash into the project (whether for the land or to bridge the gap between the funding and higher development costs) and are more likely to pay attention to a variety of aspects of the project, which can be beneficial in a wide variety of ways. For example, most lenders use the LTV ratio to help decide how much equity is needed.

Any developers who want to find equity investors should collect the relevant information on their prospective partners, such as financial resources, net worth, and investment experience. All this information should be given to a developer to give them a better idea of what a potential investor offers and whether they are suitable for the project.

When talking to family and friends about becoming investors, they must know the risks, especially if their experience in property development is limited. Try not to oversell, or they could hold you accountable for any losses.

If you want to find a good investor, we have an investor information package template that could help you. support@sherwoodfinance.com.au

7 Equity partners

A wise developer should do their best to build ongoing relationships. Many investors out there have a significant amount of cash in savings. If you convince them that your project is profitable, it can be an ideal partnership.

Developers should always have options for potential partners, and if this is the case, they have the chance to be more successful and even the ability to use their capital for future projects. It is often easier to persuade people than others, and there could be problems if any rules are not followed. Here are things you should keep in mind to reduce the chances of any problems occurring later in the partnership.

▸ You should only seek a partner when necessary, and the person joining should contribute wherever you are lacking. The best way to make the most out of a partnership is to have individuals whose skills and resources come rather than clashing.

▸ Don't form a partnership with just anyone, whether you are considering friends or business associates, several considerations before asking someone to become a partner. First, for the best possible results, you need to be selective and find someone who has experience in the industry (since failing to reach the projected returns with someone who does not know the potential risks could cause issues).

▸ To encourage an investor to lend you money for your project, you are going to need to prove to them worthwhile. Therefore, before approaching any potential partners, you must have all the information (from debt required to financial projections) laid out in a formal 'investor package'.

8 Securities

Land subdivision

One of the main reasons developers choose to build on vacant land is that a limited resource to build on that can offer an opportunity to add a significant amount of value to an empty site. Better yet, raw land can be rezoned or subdivided, so they can sell separately the separate portions of land and for a significant profit.

Many people see it as either land banking or pure land speculation. An investor will hope to hold the land with the latter until rezoning occurs. Developers will often plan out a project to improve the land and resell it.

Here are two essential factors to consider about these options; land prices can be susceptible to supply and demand, with prices skyrocketing when there's little supply and significant demand in the area. Because of these types of investments, land development can be capital intensive and is not a project that produces income for some time.

Typically, getting finance for land developments is not always a simple task because approval can rely on project income, experience, equity and more. One of the main reasons developers best investigate lenders earlier. Since this can give them a better opportunity to learn more about how different lenders feel about the project. Here is information that you should have prepared when applying for funding:

▸ The land's historical background (as well as the history of the surrounding area)

▸ An overview of the development (and any factors worth pointing out)

▸ If available, a valuation report on the land

▸ Any available information based on the market research you have done

▸ Details of your company, shareholders, etc.

▸ A list of your assets and liabilities (statement of position)

In most cases, if the timing seems right, and the project has potential, a lender will be more inclined to offer the money you need.

Depending on your plans, you could either get the land buy and construction funding as separate loans or as one. Perhaps you would instead buy the land yourself since borrowed funds reduce profit and raw land doesn't offer immediate income.

Multi-level residential flats

We rarely saw Australians living in high-rise apartments before 1970, with the only exceptions being tenants of state housing commissions or individuals in unusual areas of Sydney. In contrast, today, it's interesting to see how much more desirable it has become, because of population growth and a variety of new apartment blocks in the country's capitals. Town planners build more flats to add more life outside of work hours to a city. Plus, inner-city suburbs have become more attractive to buyers and renters over the years. If you check out the data, you see that the land values are higher in properties closer to the Central Business district.

The demand and principles of apartment buildings are like medium density housing. The potential advantages and risks are notable similarities, although several more. One way that it differs is that there are variables determining factors like equity. Consider the following.

▸ High rise is buildings with nine or more floors. Most have over 100 apartments and a minimum of one lift.

▸ Mid - rise – multi-story buildings with a lift

▸ Garden style – one to a four-story apartment building in a garden-enjoy setting.

▸ Walk up – four- to six-story apartments without a lift.

Townhouses and villas

For quite some time, townhouses and villas have been among the most common housing options across the country. Factors like affordability and changing demographics have helped to make these properties even more desirable, especially in older suburbs.

These developments will often require higher budgets and personal equity, leaving an individual vulnerable to interest rate volatility when taking out finance. In most cases, the best plan is to sell off as many units as possible before starting construction. But this is not always easy.

Office space

It is common for entire office buildings to be developed or purchased by large investment firms, not available to most investors. Therefore, office space is considered a category of commercial property. Although not to be confused with retail space, office space can often be renovated and requires a little cost to fit out compared to other commercial securities.

There can be various crucial factors to consider, like the interior layout and access for those with disabilities. Many large office buildings today also contain a café and have most necessities within close distance, which are desirable for tenants.

This often makes them an excellent base for those who need a collaborative work environment. A lease will last for three to five years, with a tenant paying all the outgoings.

Industrial and commercial properties

Buildings that offer rental space and bulk storage are often called industrial properties. They can design for large warehouses, distribution centres, storage facilities, etc. but, they typically need a small space reserved for an office.

While this type of real estate is not aesthetically pleasing, it's attractive to commercial lenders because, they can be stable and profitable assets. These types of developments are let on a net lease basis – meaning that a tenant will be required to pay some or all the outgoing costs (from property taxes to build insurance).

The industry has grown because of the consumer shift into e-commerce. These properties often do better in redeveloped urban areas (especially if aesthetics is not an issue). but, vital to consider other factors when choosing a destination, like how easy to access main transport.

Certain suburbs specialise in certain forms of industrial space, offering positions for warehouses that are close to major highways and freeways. Being near airports and shipping locations can be essential, especially for most businesses considering leasing the property. A few key considerations include office warehouses and manufacturing facilities, but many more to consider before developing.

Case Study

Industrial construction development site

Property details

Land for industrial use nearby Liverpool, New South Wales.

What the client wanted

The corporate borrowers from interstate were full of energy and wanted local banking contacts with competitive terms.

Key points

The lenders needed assurance of proven industry accomplishments as they were applying for a considerable amount of money.

Difficulties along the way

A few of the lenders we engaged had concerns about the total amount of lending they had outstanding with other financial institutions.

What we did

After arranging a meeting with a state director from a significant local lender, we offered finance at competitive terms.

The results

A competitive LVR (Loan to Value Ratio) and the interest rate resulted in a satisfied corporate interstate client.

▸ LVR: gross 70%

▸ Rate: 4% (interest only)

▸ Term: 5 years

Auction or Private Treaty

A good auction can be exciting, whether in-house or even held on a suburban street. It can become so intense that the bids can sometimes surpass expectations because of popular demand. The aim of an auction is to create a large, exciting atmosphere for the sale while also providing bidders and sellers with transparency.

If you are considering bidding at an auction, it's essential that you first set yourself a budget and a firm limit. A lender must approve your finances or in place. If you have any enquiries, contact our team.

If an auction does not meet the vendor's expectations and the last bid is declared to be insufficient by the vendor, the property will often be passed on to the highest bidder or will be reverted to a private treaty sale. The same goes for other situations, like when there are no genuine bidders.

If there are several under-bidders, the house will be passed in, and the highest bidder will have a private conversation about the vendor's reserve level. Agents are likely to tell everyone involved that there is still a chance to take the property for a higher bid, although the first bidder is given the initial right of refusal. If they're not satisfied with the reserve price, the agents can continue negotiations with under-bidders.

Deciding between an auction or private treaty often comes down to which one will produce the best results. There're circumstances when auctions can seem like the best solution. For example, several investors might outdo each other to get the property regardless of the extra money.

In Australia, private treaties sell most real estate. Vendors (sellers) decide the price at which they marketed their properties for sale under this process. If the buyer is not happy with the price, they begin negotiations by offering a lower one.

Negotiation is a natural part of buying or selling a property by private treaty. To get the highest price, a seller often looks for a private treaty sale to work like a slow-motion auction, this may take place over hours and sometimes days, weeks, or even months., offers come in and move back and forth between the seller and purchaser. Rather than taking place during a ten-minute auction with other bidders in front of the property.

A seller's agent receives the offer. When a vendor agrees to a request, they will ask the agent to accept it, and contracts are then written and exchanged. A private treaty can seem less stressful and more manageable compared to an auction sale or buy. But keep in mind that a private treaty requires more negotiation skills from the seller.

Some states require that you make an offer in writing, often by filling out a form and signing it. For example, you can put in a verbal offer in New South Wales, Queensland, and Victoria, as well as the Northern Territory and the ACT (Australian Capital Territory). Still, these are viewed more seriously if they are in writing.

We suggest following the procedure set out in your state or territory. Consider the following as a guide because local governments and buyers often scrutinise the auction process, which could change.

Victoria

Auction

At the start of the auction, there is no requirement to register your intent to bid unless a condition imposed by the real estate agency. Only the auctioneer may make a vendor bid, and they must announce a 'vendor bid.' If a co-owner intends to bid, the auctioneer must show this at the commencement of the auction. Bidders can ask during the auction if the property is 'on the market.' law prohibits Dummy bids. For mortgagee sales, Deceased estates or Family Law Matters, the property must go to auction; therefore, the agent cannot convey offers before the auction date.

Private treaty

The Estate Agents Professional Conduct Regulations 2018 state all offers must be communicated unless instructed to the contrary in writing by the vendor. Besides written submissions, buyers can also make verbal offers. If you want the vendor to take you, submit a completed contract for sale and offer a deposit. After the vendor accepts your request, your offer becomes binding only when you and the vendor exchange contracts, and a deposit (10%) is accounted for.

Tasmania

Auction

Having your finance and deposit ready on the day is essential. Vendors may bid up to the reserve price, and the auctioneer must state vendor bids to potential buyers assembled at the auction. If the offers do not reach the reserve, you may negotiate with the vendor afterwards and settle on a negotiated price. Contracts of Sale are signed and exchanged during that day. Dummy bidding is not allowed.

Private treaty

To make an offer, buyers should use the law society contract of sale provided by their agent. If you wish, you can ask your attorney or conveyancer to prepare the offer document for you. The agent must pass all offers but may not if the request is below the vendor's stipulated amount. It does not require sellers to show known defects with the property. A cooling-off period of three days. However, if both parties choose not to use it, no cooling-off period applies once the contract of sale is signed by both parties and exchanged finance proceeds.

New South Wales

Auction

To take part in or bid at a residential auction, potential buyers must register by showing identification and will be given a bidder's number. The auctioneer oversees the bidding process. The vendor sets the reserve price before the auction and is entitled to one vendor bid. If they do not reach the reserve price, the highest bidder can negotiate with the sales agent. Unless agreed before the auction, they require a ten per cent deposit at the fall of the hammer. Ensure finances are ready as they exchanged contracts on the day. Dummy bids are illegal.

Private treaty

Offers can be verbal or in writing. Although making a formal offer, the vendor is more likely to accept. When the vendor accepts your request, a five-day cooling-off period begins. They do not bound the buyers and sellers until they exchanged signed contracts. Then titles are prepared, they returned loan documentation signed. The buyer must pay a deposit. Can complete settlement process within 30 - 90 days.

Australian Capital Territory

Auction

You must register to bid by providing the real estate agent at the auction with proof of your identity, and a bidder's number is assigned. The agent can make one vendor bid on behalf of the vendor and must be stated as a vendor bid. The highest bidder must exceed the reserve price set before the auction begins. If they do not meet the reserve, the highest bidder will negotiate with the sales agent. The highest bidder will have to sign contracts and pay the agreed deposit on the day. Finance must be in place to meet settlement under absolute terms, and 'dummy bidding' is prohibited.

Private treaty

Agents must notify the vendor of all offers and cannot be made and must be in writing. The advertised price must be similar and close to what the seller will accept. The seller can receive offers from other interested parties until they exchanged contracts. The sales agent will send the contract and offer documentation to the buyer's solicitor upon accepting the offer. Once the buyer and seller have both signed and exchanged the contract, it becomes binding. The five-day cooling-off period can only be waived or amended with signed approval from the vendor.

Western Australia

Auction

Auctions are not as common in Western Australia as in other states. The auctioneer starts by detailing the benefits of the property and any relevant information and restrictions on the title. In addition, they must show the required deposit to be paid before commencing. The auctioneer then calls for or announces an opening bid below the reserve price. Offers from vendors are permitted. They must specify it in the auction form whether the seller will make bids and how many. On the fall of the hammer, the buyer will pay the agreed deposit. Contracts exchanged that day. Dummy bids are illegal.

Private treaty

If you suggest making an offer, buyers must fill out and sign an offer and acceptance contract (O & A). The agent will prepare either of the two forms, Contract for Sale of Land and General Conditions or the Strata Title, and the agent will present the offer to the vendor. The vendor may either accept or counter the offer by amending the O & A or reject it, and the agent must inform the purchaser. Once the offer is accepted, the settlement must occur within the agreed timeframe.

Queensland

Auction

Before the auction begins, you must register with the auctioneer. They will offer a number paddle. Until the reserve price, vendor bids can be accepted, provided the auctioneer announces them in the conditions of sale at the beginning of the auction. Auctioneers cannot take false bids. After the auction, contracts are signed, and they pay a five to ten per cent deposit.

Private treaty

Agents can list prices over the minimum the vendor will accept. but, agents are prohibited from listing below the vendors' minimum price, often considered bait advertising an offence. Verbal offers can be made, and they must send all written offers to the vendor. When your offer is accepted, the agent must offer you with a contract of sale, accompanied by a warning statement. The purchaser will need to pay a deposit after the five-day cooling-off period. This takes between 30 two 90 days for settlement.

South Australia

Auction

You must register by providing your identification to the agent conducting the sale. For someone else to bid on your behalf, you will need to offer proof of your identity plus a signed authorisation letter. They usually set a reserve price, in writing, before the auction. You should know the vendor is entitled to three bids. The vendor bids must not exceed the reserve price. The auctioneer must announce each such bid as a 'vendor bid'. If reported throughout the auction, it shows. The vendor's reserve price is not reached. If you are the highest bidder and the reserve price is not met, you can negotiate. At the fall of the hammer, the successful bidder must pay a ten per cent deposit. It would be best if you had your finance ready because they exchange contracts on the day. Dummy bids are not allowed.

Private treaty

All offers must be in writing that discloses the seller's name, contact information, the price, the settlement date, and any other conditions. Each submission can include a date by which the offer lapses. Before a vendor accepts an offer, the agent must make sure the vendor has received all written offers. Requests are often subject to building inspection and loan approval or any other conditions by the purchaser or vendor. Both parties must sign a contract of sale before the offer is binding. To complete the settlement, it can take from 30 to 90 days.

Northern Territory

Auction

On the day, the auctioneer will detail the terms and conditions of the auction process and then call for bids on the property. All bidders must register by showing identification. The Auctioneers must not engage in conduct that is fraudulent or misleading. Dummy bids are prohibited. Before the auction, the vendor will set a 'reserve price', and they will pass the property in unless the bidding reaches that point. An auctioneer will often tell the attendees that the property is 'on the market', showing it has passed the reserve price and will be sold to the highest bidder. If they do not reach the reserve, bidders negotiate with the selling agent. As usual, ensure that finance is ready to meet the agreed settlement date.

Private treaty

An offer on a property should be on a formal contract, although buyers can make verbal offers, and they must send all offers to the vendor. The vendor is not bound to accept your submission until the contract of sale is exchanged. At the time of the exchange, the purchaser must pay a deposit. The settlement process can take from 30 to 90 days.

In conclusion

It is vital to find an experienced finance broker in commercial lending. This is because they act as an intermediary between a developer and investor. Finding a quality broker is ideal for several reasons, from their relationships with banks and financial institutions to their services in negotiating loan terms with third parties. Sometimes, a brokerage with their experience could even be a lender and offer funding. But they have all the expertise they need to offer the perfect balance for their clients.

While many residential brokerages will say that they work with commercial transactions, it's wise to go with a team that specialises in commercial finance. So be cautious with companies that upsell their products, as they may not focus on providing you with the best possible service. Although many commercial lenders deal with brokers, always wise to take your time to find an experienced broker. A reliable broker should be upfront about the shortcomings of different deals and entry and exit costs.

It can be worth noting that not all brokerages know all market sectors, so you should always ask about what they offer and where their area of expertise lies. It is wise to ask how they package a loan application since any good broker will take extra care to package the proposal and work around issues they come across. Many brokerage companies will also work with title companies, property valuers and other professionals whose expertise could come in handy. They should also know when to dispute a refusal or low valuation and which lenders to go to next if negotiations fail.

If you seek finance, contact our team to find out more, as it could make all the difference. Without finance, there may not even be a project. Suppose you are hoping to become a property developer. In that case, you must try to learn about how financing works and a variety of other factors, like negotiating with banks (since not always as simple as it may seem). We could help you find a worthwhile lender in no time at all. We have worked with several over the years and have met many who can offer great funding options for various needs, no matter how obscure or unique the project in question may be. Consider looking at our website for more information. Contact us.

Arrangement fees

When lenders charge for the effort of providing financing to a borrower, this fee can vary from one lender to another.

Auction

An auctioneer conducts a sales process in public.

Auctioneer

A profession that oversees the sale of real estate or other items whereby persons become purchasers by competition in public view, the sale favours the highest bidder.

Australian Bureau of Statistics

A federal statutory agency, the Australian Bureau of Statistics (ABS), collects and analyses statistical data and provides evidence-based advice to federal, state and territory governments.

Business activity statements (BAS)

BAS is used to reconciling the tax collected by a business is known as Good and Services Tax (GST), paid to the government monthly, quarterly, or annually.

Balance

A statement begins with your last statement's balance, which is the amount you had within your account at the end of the previous report.

Bankruptcy

A legal concept that you would be best to avoid. Also known as Insolvency, this occurs when an individual cannot meet their financial obligations within a reasonable time frame or if their liabilities exceed their assets.

Bid

A method of purchasing real estate at auction is by an offering.

Caveat

A property caveat is a claim to a property as a legal document. Creating a caveat allows both parties to claim their share of interest. Until the caveat is settled, no further transactions can be registered against the title.

Capital Gains Tax

If you sell an asset such as investment property for a profit, you are subject to capital gains tax (CGT). At the end of the fiscal year, they add the capital gain to your income tax.

Cheque

Cheques detail any amount of money that's withdrawn since account holders often write the cheque to pay someone. This includes the number on the cheque and the amount taken out.

Court judgement

If a person cannot repay their creditors, creditors can get a judgment in court.

Commercial tenants

Commercial, industrial, and retail properties are standard in arranging long-term leases. In addition, outgoings are negotiated but passed onto the tenant.

Commitment fee

They add a fee onto a loan to compensate a lender for their commitment to offering to fund.

Company secretary

A secretary's responsibility is to circulate agendas and other documents to directors, shareholders, and auditors and make correct minutes of shareholder and directors meetings and resolutions.

Contract of sale

An agreement includes the terms, conditions signed, dated and witnessed by all related parties.

Conveyance

When real estate is transferred from one party to another, in real estate, this could be when a seller transfers the ownership of a property to a buyer.

Collateral

Collateral is protection to mitigate the risks involved with lending.

Credit

While this refers to several aspects of lending, most used to describe a contract agreement where an individual receives money and repays the lender by a predetermined date (usually with an additional interest fee).

Credit score

Used by lenders to decide whether to accept funding applications based on the risk associated with the borrower. Also referred to as a credit rating.

Development Approval

Local town planning authorities offer written approval for a project, prepared by the developer's or landowner's consultants, allowing the project to move forward as per the development plan.

Deposit

The amount of money needed to be paid upfront as part of the loan agreement. The amount specified can often vary depending on a variety of circumstances.

Division of Property

fair distribution, or property division, divides property rights and obligations between divorced or De facto spouses and business partners.

Director

An individual that manages a company's operations, with the ability to exercise the business' powers for whatever needs it may have.

Economy

A summary of goods, services produced, distributed and sold within a region or country.

Equity

Property equity is the difference between the remaining debt and the asset's capital value in question.

Exchange of Contracts

When a seller and buyer sign a copy of the sale contract and then exchange these documents, create a binding agreement for the sale of real estate on agreed terms. They then bound the parties to proceed to settlement, subject to any cooling-off period that may apply.

First mortgage

When a borrower uses the property as security for the first time as collateral for a loan, as usual, if they do not meet the mortgage repayments as agreed, the lender can seize the security.

Financial position

An organisation's financial position refers to its assets, liabilities, and equity balances. In a broader sense, the concept can describe the financial condition, which is determined by analysing and comparing its financial statements.

GSA (General Security Agreement)

They register GSAs on a National Register to secure the lender's interest against the relevant security entity/ asset. As part of the Register, lenders can also negotiate a priority system to ensure that their interests are protected and prioritised.

Guarantor

In property development transactions, lenders could require additional security to reduce their risk should the developer default on a loan. This guarantee can take various forms, from cash to property.

Gross Realised Value

In property construction, the Gross Realisation Value is the gross sales (or GST exclusive value of the property) upon the completion of the project. Also known as GRV.

Initial Public Offering

When a company raises capital from public investors by offering shares of a corporation in a public share issuance, we often abbreviate it to IPO.

Interest rate

The amount of interest charged on a loan, in proportion to the amount borrowed, allows a bank or lender to profit when distributing funds.

Investment property

A real estate buy intends to earn rental income or capital gain.

Indicative offer

Lenders often show or suggest that the offer may proceed if they meet conditions, also known as a conditional offer.

Joint and severally

Where all parties are equally accountable for the full terms of the agreement, they have entered. For example, in a personal liability case, each party will pursue to repay the entire amount owed.

Land tax

Whether you own or jointly an investment property, you will pay land tax. The amounts vary from state to state.

Lawyer

A lawyer is someone who practices law and deals with legal issues. A lawyer provides legal advice and represents people in court.

Land Banking

Usually refers to financing secured for the acquisition and holding of developmental sites with no certainty of rapid development.

Legal fees

Upon completing the buy, the solicitor or conveyancer will charge a fee for the legal work carried out during buying. Most solicitors charge a flat fee regardless of the property's value.

Letter of Offer

When a lender issues a finance offer to a borrower, it can be accepted or rejected depending on the borrower in question acceptance.

Lease agreements

They make lease agreements between the property owner and tenant to occupy real estate.

Loan to Value Ratio

All lenders use a Loan to Value Ratio to assess risk when they consider funding and can have a tremendous impact on the terms offered, abbreviated to LTV (loan to values) or LVR (Loan to Value Ratio).

Litigation

When disputes are resolved in court through litigation, unless the parties settle before trial, a judge may make the final decision for the parties in litigation.

Liabilities

Liabilities are obligations between two parties that have not yet been completed or repaid.

Mortgage

A debt passed onto a borrower from a lender secured by a property.

Mortgagee sale

In the event of a default by the mortgagor, the mortgagee claims the security and resells to avoid economic losses.

Mortgagor

A borrower (individual or company) has an interest in a property through a mortgage as security for credit advancement.

Net Realised Value

They reduced the asset value realised on the sale because of standard deductions. Therefore, it is often abbreviated to NRV.

Non-conforming loans

The term non-conforming loan refers to lending that does not meet the criteria for bank financing. There are a variety of reasons for this.

Non-recourse loan

When a lender can seize the security if a borrower defaults on their payments, the difference from standard scenarios is that the lender cannot get further compensation, even if the collateral covers the total unpaid loan.

Offshore

Ideal for overseas investors, most offshore financing options are available for competitive prices and offer enticing sums of money. The general, the applications to be considered are company borrowers.

Passed in

If the owner's reserve price has not been met and they do not sell a property at auction; therefore, passed in.

Periodic lease

Typical with residential, a tenant continues to rent and occupy the property beyond the expiration of the lease agreement.

Private treaty sale

The terms and conditions of a private sale between a seller and buyer to buy the real estate vary from state to state.

Presales

A lender will want a certain number of presales to reduce their risks. While the percentage of pre-sold units is not set, funding can vary slightly from one lender to another.

Principal and interest mortgage

A standard mortgage, with the difference that monthly repayments are part capital and part interest.

Property Acquisition

When legal ownership or rights over real estate are transferred, the rules may vary from one state to another.

Property Maintenance

Property owners will need to decide about building works and maintenance. The agent managing your property will manage and looking after the property. This includes marketing your property, collecting rent and fixing any issues.

Progress Payments

As the construction progresses, lenders drawdown payments in stages. Therefore, the lender needs to report the work completed by its Quantity Surveyor to compare the completed work as part of the loan agreement.

Property Settlement

A legal process facilitated by the legal and financial representatives of the purchaser and the seller. Settlement occurs when ownership is passed from the seller to the buyer. Typically, the settlement date is determined in the contract of sale by the vendor.

Profit

When the financial earnings of a business activity exceed the amount needed for the costs, taxes, etc., this could be when a company buys something and sells it for a higher price.

Preferred equity

Investments or loans exceeding the level associated with project and deemed debt but not taking part in equal ranking equity.

Rescind

To discontinue a contract of sale.

Reserve Price

The vendor agrees upon the minimum acceptable price before the Auction.

Residential tenants

In most cases, residential leases last for one year; any shorter would be costly for the property owner for re-tenanting costs such as marketing, rental income delays and re-letting fees to the agent.

Recourse

If the debt obligation is not honoured, a lender may get a borrower's security. A full recourse is when a lender can take additional assets to repay the entire unpaid debt.

Receipt

A note of any money that is deposited into your account. It also known as paid-in or credits.

Reserve Bank of Australia

The Australian central bank publishes and controls monetary policy. This can have a varying, underlying effect on mortgage rates.

Settlement Date

The last part of the process is whereby the purchaser completes the payment of the contract price to the seller, and they transferred legal possession to the purchaser.

Share certificates

A share certificate is a document that is issued by a company that sells shares. An investor receives a share certificate upon purchasing a certain number of shares and as a record of ownership.

Stamp duty

All Australian States and Territories impose stamp duty. The amount varies from state to state. Taxes on business purchases differ from taxes on real estate. It arises from the sale or transfer of a wide range of personal and business assets.

Joint tenants

Joint tenancy is the default type of shared ownership. There is no property division between the joint owners; each owns one hundred per cent of the property. Legal ownership of the property passes to the surviving joint owner when a joint owner dies.

Statement of Position

According to their assets and liabilities, companies or individual positions show the current net equity position.

Security

Security on a mortgage is essential because it reduces the risk a lender takes on when providing a loan. Suppose a loan is backed by property, for example. Then, if the borrower defaults on repayments, the lender may seize the property to claim the outstanding debt.

Share certificates

Whenever a company sells shares on the market, it issues shares certificates. As proof of ownership and as a record of the purchase, they issue shares certificates to shareholders.

Shareholders

A person or business that owns a share in a company's stock. They can receive capital gains, take capital losses, and they may receive dividend payments. They are equity owners and have the same benefits and drawbacks as Directors.

Second mortgage

A borrower can offer their real estate as collateral a second time to another lender while the first still has finance secured. As a result, the subsequent lender takes a second charge over the property.

Senior Debt

The registered mortgage holds the property's first ranking for a primary mortgage or principal debt. Developers often prefer senior debt as the margins are lower since banks or significant mortgage funds typically offer senior debt.

Tax returns

Tax authorities use this process to assess a taxpayer's liability based on their annual income personal circumstances and include corporate entities.

Tenants in common

A joint ownership arrangement exists when mulitple individuals own the same property, but neither has the right of one hundred per cent ownership of the property. For example, if you do not make a will, you can "will" your share of the property to a beneficiary of your choice.

Valuer

A company appointed to conduct the assessment of the current market value of the real estate.

Variation

To change or alter the conditions of the contract of sale.

Valuation

Not to be confused with make sure an appraisal, as a valuation provides a more correct and recognised property value.

Vendor

In a real estate transaction, a person(s) or entity sells the property.

Quantity Surveyor

A qualified individual that examines costs associated with the building costs. Market conditions impact labour costs and material suppliers with the DA (development approval). Lenders also keep them to make sure that the project is correctly costed.

Yield

A sign of income by percentage earned on real estate. It is Calculated by the received net income and the market value of the real estate.

Zoning

The local council planning controls current and future development, including residential, business, and industrial uses.

**For further information
about Sherwood Finance:**

Call us 1800 743 796

head to the website
www.sherwoodfinance.com.au

follow us on Facebook, Instagram
and Twitter.